Intellectual Suicide

Poetry
to Die For

Crystophver R

GARDEN OAK PRESS
Rainbow, California

gardenoakpress.com

Garden Oak Press
1953 Huffstatler St., Suite A
Rainbow, CA 92028
760 728-2088
gardenoakpress.com
gardenoakpress@gmail.com

© Crystophver R   All rights reserved

No part of this book may be reproduced, stored in a retrieval system or transmitted by any means without the express written consent of the Publisher.

First published by Garden Oak Press on June 15, 2019

ISBN-13:   978-1-7323753-3-8

Printed in the United States of America

The views expressed in this collection of poems are solely those of the poet and do not necessarily reflect the views of the Publisher and the Publisher hereby disclaims any responsibility for them.

To many who shall remain nameless

These are another few who have enriched my journey:

Indian Magique, The Mightier P.E.N.S. (Poetical Expeditionary Nation of Semanticists) William Shakespeare, Peter Brook, Ken & Barbara Parks, Jean & Stan Johnson, Cheyenne, Liz, Autumn, & Zoey Roze, Tori & Jody Roze, Somer & Mike Roze-Post, Fearless Fran Gilhooly, Thomas J. Simitzes, Judy Mullenix, John David Peters, Ralph Steadman, Bernard Baldan, Jack See, Hugh Monahan, Frank Muhr, Joseph T. Drew, Wm. R. Franklin, Barbara Wilson, Sally Brown, Mark Wenzel, Tavis & J. Michael Ross, Lee & Geoff Clark, Randy, Daniel, Deborah Mae, Noah, Kari, Amy & Stephen Parks, Michael (Izzy Blaze) Turner, Chris Vannoy, Rudy G, Pat Andrus, Steve Haralson, TLaLoc Rodriguez, Milton Woodruff, Arthur J. Noll, Bob Yarber, George Loveland, Minerva Marquis, Zopilote, Todd Gloria, Lewis Higgins, Karl Kramer, Kristi Fenick, Kathy Aceves, Stacey LoMedico, Tammy Brooks, Sinthya Carranza, Jim Moreno, Seretta Martin, Adam Greenfield, Sylvia Isely-Aguilera, Jenifer Whisper, Helen Loveland, Bobby Larsen, Laurie Lehmann-Gray, Sharyn Noll, Charlie Berigan, Susan Walter, A.M. Charlens, Sam Woodhouse, Douglas Jacobs, Darla Cash, Sandra Abbott ,Michael O'Mahony, C.R.A.S.H.,

and everyone I pray for. You know who you are. Add your name if you remember when our lives have touched…

Contents

The End	3
I Only Came for the Poetry	4
Apro-Poetry	5
A Letter to My Children	6
Hey Man	7
The Tooth of Truth	8
That Family of Mine	9
The Alzheimer's Embers of November	10
Got a Solution?	11
I Caught That Glimpse	12
If You Leave Now	14
Bipolar Love	15
Help Me Find My Sister	16
Thanking You Forever . . .	17
Friskin' the Whiskers	18
American Royalty	20
Gloria	21
What Price Glory?	24
A Pirate's Ditty	25
Rose O.D.	26
Butts on Bicycles	27
Diaspora Smack-Down	28
What?	29
The Dying of the Light & The Year of Promised Fright	30
A Dish for the Gods	33
Smoke 'Em If You've Got 'Em	34
your eyes betray your words	35
I Told You So!	36
Big House Blues	39
Dancing	40
Amber Sound Flow Freely	41
Get What You Need	42
Red Rover, Red Rover, Let October Be Over	44
Nickle-Bag Reality	46
Jizz What You Want	47
The Saga of Brother Rat	48
What Is Change?	50
Cell Phone Eavesdropping	51
Auld Lang Synge	52
Boneroo Wood	53
Kiss Another One Good-Bye	54

Hunni-Do Fixes the World!	55
All That Fuss	56
Godsending Gerunding	57
Never Will Be Forever	58
Reading the Seeds	60
A Fine-Tuned Machine	61
The Seven Veils of Crisis	62
`O Behave, or Not OB	64
No Twix, Santa's Tweet	65
This Party Sucks!	66
A Pilgrimage of Love	67
Recovering from Life	68
Earthbound Astrologers	69
Intellectual Suicide	70
Wait Station Earth	73
Mercutio, King of Cats	74
No Leg to Stand On	76
Solipsist-Station	78
Bored Shortz	79
"It's All Right!"	80
A Kiss	81
The Earth Sucks	82
Perfection Is What Is. . .	83
Hallow Greetings	84
Malice of Forethought	86
The Rise and Fall of It All	87
The Covenant of Light	88
Zeugma in Action	90
Seeking Comfort	91
Indian Magique	92
Subconsciously Bogart	95
Born Out of Darkness	96
The Warm Bus	97
Gift Exchange	98
Seized by the Moment	100
Words	101
The Book of: I-Say-Ah, One-Four-All	102
While Old Wounds Bleed	103
One Eternal Moment	104
Angels Take Flight	105
From the Mire	108

You Know Better Than I	109
Light-Blind and Abandoned	110
Saint Jude's Prayer	111
You Were Once	112
Death Becomes Us	113
The Daily Bread Excursion	114
Every Word's a Prayer	119
ABOUT THE POET	120
CREDITS	122
ACKNOWLEDGEMENTS	123

Intellectual Suicide

**Poetry
to Die For**

To Kathleen

My wish, to issue you Poetic License, to operate and navigate a peacefully prolific journey, shedding the fear, guilt, and shame of Intellectual Suicide, in pursuit of life, liberty, and The Poetry of Life…

God Bless,
Christopher R

Crystophver R

The End

The End begins again
no matter where you leave it

It will start
without any conscious
effort or design

The End is an extension
of an endless
chain of breaths
connecting lifetimes
to central
nervous systems
of living thoughts
that await
the beholder
of meaningful
moments

The End is near

just this side

of New Beginnings

I Only Came for the Poetry

I only came for the poetry,
to pay homage to the symmetry,
naturalistically absurd,
I ain't here for no games,
only to get off on the words,
while slappin' some skin and droppin' the names
to the primal rhythms of heavy breath,
undressing the night of diaphanous day,
passions reborn from a climax-like death,
laid out and stiff in sweet metered grooves,
sticky wet stanzas squirt, gush, and seep,
in locked lyrical rapture from floor to the rooves
metaphors drip, throb strophic and deep.

As we float back to our senses,
stagger up off the roof, walls, and floor,
straighten our ties and our tenses,
and, without so much as a haiku, head for the door.

Apro-Poetry

Words fail all descriptions of the poetry of life.
The turning smile,
the secret glance,
have no comparisons in transcribed thoughts,
as they trace wind shadows
across the face of ages,
we watch the ships come and go.

There is no recounting
for this poetry of life.
You have to be here,
and feel the scorching sun
within your heart,
the rocking earth
within your soul.

Build your towers to heaven,
and talk to God, straight across.

No one else can write your poem,
nor live each stanza as you do.

This is your pilgrimage,
through moment and perception,
crying out for meaning,
and impatiently making up your own.

A Letter to My Children

I am practiced in the imperfect art of making family,
giving and taking what I had, with painful pleasure,
drowned in self-absorption, bottomed out in fetal surrender.
A salmon dream, returning home,
to consummate a covenant,
of recycled visions in food chain precisions.
Remember that dream we dreamed,
                                  growing up and doing right,
in stereotyped ideals? Someday? Did you forget?
Did you think it would all be different? All the same,
you got just enough, today and now.
Life's decisions made never knowing
ever going, always growing seeds are sowing…

What did you decide?
I almost forgot, you don't have to decide!
This is America!
You have the right to remain silent, and take it in the shorts!
Ain't no never mind; never ever can become forever.

Don't do what I did! Learn your role!
Just like in the movies, "Take one!"
If you don't get it right, "Take two!"
All those missed "takes." Do it 'til you get it right!
Don't give up!!!
That's how you're supposed to do it; learn by my mistakes!
Do what you want! Until you have children.
Then you have to figure in the wants of others.
What do we want? Do what you want, when we want!
Want it! Work with it! Make it happen! Get it!
Pass it on! You've got the tools!
Trust in the cycle!
Keep your word, don't take it personally, or make
assumptions,
and always do your best!
This is my prayer. Pass it on...

Hey Man

Hey Man!
Hey!
Yeah Man, You!
Man?

Hey Man,
Can You Hear Me?

Wake Up Man!

    Listen!

    The Earth Is Devouring You!
    Rise Up, Man!
    Life Will Leave You For Another!
    Move Man!
    Your Dreams Will Lie Barren!
    Your Work, Tears, Cries, Jeers…
    Wasted!
    Hey Man!
    Man?
    Can You Hear Me?
    Man?

The Tooth of Truth

How stately doth the truth compare
to any words that man can bear
in his excuse for deed or thought,
or, being caught, where he should not
                have sought to tread.

Panic tortures one to give
feeble excuse for why he lives,
or dies, or hurts, or robs,
or why it's right;

        or, "I'm just doing my job!"

While something suffers in that attempt
in the placing of one's contempt,
in a path that would preempt the truth,
and further tempt a man from what he does,
or what he was,
or if his cause helps us all,
or, if it's meant for man's downfall.

One more change was needed,
before the die was cast,
something strange proceeded
to make this change the last.

Lifting eyes toward heaven;
he began to look within,
and see the truth for what it told him,

        disrespect is our only sin.

That Family of Mine

That family of mine drives up in a can,
looking quite suspect, like a large can of SPAM.
And if you ask them, they don't give a damn,
what you thought, or you ought,
what you're taught, or you bought,
what you are, or you're not.
They just want what you got.

They want what they want, but don't know what it is.
Don't give a crap, and gotta go whiz;
they know it all, so's mind your own biz!

They've done it all, and they'll do it again.
They'll write you off, just give 'em a pen.
Run you right over, do you right in,
seal up your fate, condemn you to sin.

Trash up your house, soil up your sheets,
then kick your dog, and eat all your eats.

And when they're all done, they'll drive away,
and you'll chase them down, and beg them to stay.
'Cuz you're one of them, and can't stand the pain,
of being alone, one more year, once again.

The Alzheimer's Embers
of November

A nova to remember flickers in my mind, this truth unkind,
the rotting winds unwind.
Forgetful, forgotten, sealed memories, all naught, gone sooner;
there is no later.
Life will no longer cater to my whims,
they've all dried up, like September to December.
It's getting cold, this growing old.
The worst is yet to come. . .
Let's party and die hearty, and make our exit tardy
like the demented smarties life makes of us all.

I meant to do it later, but forgot the way,
and lost another day, in all I do and say.
But you know, that's OK, I'm getting old,
and as long as I do what I'm told, I can stay,
in the corner of my mind, feeling left behind,
by the parade of short-sighted idiots, who remind me.
Get it!? They re-mind me!
Like a tire store, they retread my head,
change my thinking, re-spin my balance,
and take away the challenge,
of two thoughts making sparks,
                in what once was a brilliant beam;
then parked in the warehouse of my woes,
                where no one knows.
But I can sit and chat about the weather;
if I can still see the light of day. . .
Where is the rage? Stay in your cage! Just act your age!
Those memories will fade. . . They will all soon be gone,
and I won't be in anybody's way, anymore.
That's what nobody's talking about!
But don't mind me. I'm just ramblin' on.
Take me no heed, I've gone to seed.
                It's just my Alzheimer's actin' up.
Be thankful you're not like me; yet. . .

Got a Solution?

What's the problem?

Got a solution?

No problem...

If you can't fix it,
find someone who can!

Quit your whining,
denying that
you're not the solution

to the economy,
social injustice,
and pollution!

This is a democracy,
is it not?

Then your problem
is our problem!

We never have any
problem
identifying problems!

If you think about it,
everything's
a potential problem!

What are we going to do,
about it?

I Caught That Glimpse

And then one day you find yourself in the mirror,
disturbed from the slumber of your life-dream.
You squint and contort your reflection into focus.
There you are, staring back into my soul;
an old stranger, a somewhat familiar face,
with tired eyes.

Don't look too closely, you'll get lost
in a flood of memories
you don't have the time to remember,
even if you could.

We look so much alike;
but still,
I feel so different
than you appear. . .

Just try to look away!

Like magnetic north,
I'm drawn back into your gaze,
that scary stare of recognition,
that rides from here to
where no one knows, or cares. . .

It's too late!

I'm locked
in that confirming stare,
that shock of reassuring terror,
strange comfort.

You remind me of someone
I used to know,

now unfamiliar,
as if we're long cast adrift. . .

I once knew someone like you,
who ran to hide amidst
the clutter of distractions,
hoping to go unnoticed,
until the surprise of their demise.

That must be what this is,
recognition for time served;
lost in the tracks of habits,
well-worn, out of service
to our cause.

Fascination overwhelms
my catatonic self,
as I obsess through recollection,
of a random keepsake
in revival…

Some dim moment
of abandoned promise…

I know I left it lying
close by.

I almost had it!

Oh, please!

Let me find it,
before I have to go. . .

It can't be far!

I've traveled all this way. . .

Why do you stare?!

If You Leave Now

If you leave now, you'll be unprepared.
You might have to hurry.
At least you won't be late. Soon you'll be, "The late-great!"
(Maybe not so late, not so great)

You'll miss all the fun.
Things could be better. You'll see new places.
Get away from it all, and rest. The sights you'll see!

Nobody on your nerves. No more complaints,
or clocks to watch, need of tolerance, or self-restraints.

You'll learn new customs, speak new languages,
think new thoughts, or try, and maybe, learn to fly.
You'll have a good time!

You will be missed.
We'll wonder how you are, what you're doing,
                              where you went, and how far.
We'll wonder if you think of us. And remember
                              all the times we had.
How you dressed, combed your hair,
                    what you liked and disliked,
how you laughed, and got embarrassed about stuff.
What made you happy, and got you so mad,
when you were hurt, and the goodness that you had.

What you did or didn't do,
          and the differences that made you you.

Somewhere in the future those little pieces of life
weave into the tapestry of a night canopied sky.
Our gaze turns upward, attracted to one star,
overwhelmed with memories, and in epiphanic unison
we declare, "There you are!"

Looking back at life, and all that it has been,
we find ourselves back together, once again. . .

Bipolar Love

Love is: grand, stupid, scary, real, obsessive, illogical, exotic,
erotic, chaotic, despotic, epizootic, hypnotic,
                                  idiotic, narcotic, neurotic,
patriotic, pathetic, psychotic, quixotic, painfully boring,
unattainable, everything, everywhere, embarrassing, revealing,
concealing, receptive, deceptive, contrived, derived,
treasured, measured, pleasured, perfectly flawed,
manipulated, over-rated, chrome plated, x-rated,
translated, negated, vacated, regulated, outdated,
quaint, modern, passé, fake, piece of cake,
shared, stolen, squandered, lost, found,
forgotten, neglected, given, taken, bestowed,
forced, wasted, excessive, unrequited, abandoned,
inspirational, hidden, extravagant, repulsive, alive, dead,
foolish, encompassing, engaging, constructive,
destructive, educational, heavy, light, free,
controlling, tough, gentle, indifferent,
durable, forever, never-ending, whatever;
frost-maker, ice breaker, dream shaper,
blue, red, pink, black and white,
nurturing, thoughtful, heart-felt,
hurtful, wrong,
a blinding, unkind, refined, divine, sublime, crime,
confining the rhyme-timing
of life sentences
longer than spans
of that eternal bliss,
that sometimes miss the kiss,
of this paralysis;

if that ain't love,

what is?

Help Me Find My Sister

Help me find my sister, she's scared and run away,
she whispered me her death wish, and vanished that same day.
Someone told her stories, that made her hope for more,
and hid the light of truth, of what was held in store.

She felt her way through darkness, and crept up to the door,
unexpectedly it opened, and the slashing pain it tore.
It destroyed her frail honesty, and made her life a lie,
standing in the silence she gently tried to die.

Her heart grew brittle, splintering in one frozen silent scream.
There she stood trembling in her finely shattered dream.

She never had a chance, believing life was kind.
Feeding on her virtues, the truth began to grind,
squeezing out her innocence, making her life's whore,
to betray a loving pureness, to wipe a bleeding sore.

Help me find my sister, I fear she's been betrayed,
by the myths we teach our daughters,
                              that cause their dreams to stray.
Help me find my sister, she's scared and run away.
She whispered me her death wish and vanished that same day.

Thanking You Forever...

What did I thank you for today?
For your smile?
Or, the while you spent with me?
How about the pleasure of your company?
Was it for the feeling of repose,
that overwhelmed me, as it rose
from within my secret thoughts
to show my outward admiration
for your presence in my life?
My load lightens
as you brighten every day.
And I am heightened in my journey
as I stray toward a light more blinding
than understanding holds,
and comprehension molds meaning
to what "I am" can be,
as we pause to flirt with infinity.
I surrender to a thankful world
that ever swirled
this moment into meaning,
that only we can share,
if we dare to know
it was meant to be
as it befalls to you and me.
"I am" at one,
thanking you, forever...

Friskin' the Whiskers

We be glammin' the Apple,
cruisin' the land o' darkness,
checkin' the main kicks at the Apollo
to mitt poundin' resound,
jivin' with the jitterbugs and jazzy jeffs,
and kickin' it killer-diller,
'til I lamped a chick in a lead sheet,
latched onto her licks;
I'm dreamin' my main queen.

She spiked on the hitch;
muggin' so smugly she hit me for 'a light,
and shot me that hip hinty glance,
I knew I was cooked,
then dealt her my prop,
"Nix out that flat-Jack!"
"Let's jam to the groove!"
"Score lily-whites, and lock up some hype!"
"Frisk up some whiskers!"

"Neigho pops!" she cooed,
"Not 'til you show me your roll!"
"Then I'll rock you 'til bright!"
The burn in her glims stiffin'd my drive;
I fished in my mouse and dug for the dimes,
spoutin', "I got the give for your take!"
She flaunts me her 'tude,
"Beat it out to the eights,
I'll roll you out in a crate!"
We danced 'til we dropped,
schemin' the dream
poppin' a horizontal bop.

Then, night leaked out the bright.

Whipped up and out,
I woke with a choke,
threw a rod, and my wad,
went into the ditch,
spent the event,
smoked by the bitch…
The come-on was gone.

I trilly, and cut out 'a the joint,
bringin' it down
I busted the point,
focused it out,
and latched on the dig;
like I, totally clambaked that gig.

American Royalty

American Royalty bastards of Hamilton and Paine,
crowned in the glory of ordain and restrain,
united and fused by circumstance and respect,
of a nation migration of cause and effect,

west of the Atlantic and a history of strife,
new hopes and new deals, seemingly rife.
Tainted torment, and exploited by greed,
hording all riches beyond the grasp to exceed.

Freedom is wealth, and deserves a fair shake,
and reaches its limit when that's all that one makes.
Some more equal than others, in the land of the free
stampede for the prize that can crush what could be.

A pact with the devil, to get what we want,
discount freedom to keep it relevant,
earned by toil, sweat, and its warrants,
slave dreams redacted by tyrants.

We soon forget the debts no one recalls
owed to our comrades who helped tear down the walls
of oppression, greed, and deceit,
sowing seeds of compassion, the union's complete,
creating a oneness, of purpose and cause,
accepting the values of God-given laws.

Taken for granted these lives that we live,
American Royalty comes at a great cost,
liberties atrophy, nothing's to give,
our wealth has been squandered and lost.

Gloria

An actress for all ages, legendary glory,
in her decline the guardian of deep mysteries,
veiled encounters, conquestial splendors,
rendezvous at Xanadu.

My tale is of a pilgrimage.
She chose me from all others,
for ritual acts of love,
upon her altar of sacrificial offering.

Undressing me with praise,
the blush of adoration,
and seductive whispers of greatness.
She took me for her throne,
praised me to exaltation,
climbed to the pinnacle of perfection,
and with the laying on of hands,
blessed, baptized and anointed.
Then, mounting on high,
she laid claim, and vanquished
my consecrated, throbbing offering. . .

I was translated by greatness,
crowned with station and new privilege,
as her minion, muse, and confidant.

She transfigured to goddess!
I pander to step lively
for her every whim and fancy.
Serving to be her lover,
surrendering a passion
of shattered gravity.

continued

Surviving the audition.
Rehearsals played into performance,
lines and cues found meaning deep within
the reality of the moment,
through a fog of breathless, sweating dedication
leading to well-practiced dramatic climaxes.

Each entrance encored an exit
from command performances
of steaming surreal scenes of passion,
conflicted, complicated, confessions,
melting into endless re-takes of erotic recall;
probing painful scrutiny,
torturing every motive, subtext, and intent,
further blurring the veil between life and apparition,
exhausting into numbing breakdowns and uncertainty.

Thoughts, dreams, emotions, and my very soul
fall subject to her mesmerizing powers,
seized and prized
as trophy and testament
to her opus empire.

Life drifts beyond recognition,
her siren calls lure me closer to her shores;
rigid in fear and anticipation
I fuse my soul to the mainmast
in token resistance.

Like a legendary colossal goddess,
with undulating arms,
and bulging breasts,
she beckons closer,
never ready to retire
the shrouding past;
alluring in assurance
of every vamping angle
and position of delight. . .

Her nightmarish image dances still,
flickering like a banshee,
on the fading silver screen
of my illusions;

crossing to my quivering threshold,
lashed to her undulating form,
securely bound in captivity...

Pressing heavy lips into my ear,
she murmurs moistly,
"I'm ready for my close-up..."

What Price Glory?

There's a pocket-sized replica of you,
sitting on someone's shelf,
just waiting to be realized.

The race is on!
Where are you hiding yourself?
Whose rules are you playing by?
Stop!
Take a beating! It's your turn!
Don't try to blame someone else,
you were next in line!
Come on!
You've got to grow up sometime!

Just about the time you get it all figured out,
something changes!

You should have read the fine print.
It happens all the time.
Have's got something,
Have not's use to have something;
what's the difference?

There is none!

Just keep trying to tell yourself that.

Remember,

the deeper you sink,
the less superficial they'll say you are. . .

A Pirate's Ditty

There's a little pirate in us all
who seems to hear that faint call
of open seas, and uncharted lands,
flying ships, and thieving hands,
'a swarming lot of blood-thirsty plotters,
o're bounding decks, 'cross deadly waters.

We are the pirates of our own dreams,
by dead reckoning, we chart our schemes,
we rob and pillage at our pleasures,
riches, jewels, and ancient treasures.

We wreck our ships on distant shores,
and bury fortunes, booties galore,
left unguarded and abandoned,
on forgotten islands, and deep-sea canyons.

Come sail away, fill our ranks,
join our band, or walk our planks!
Take no prisoners, give no thanks,
seize what we please, make merry pranks!

We live to rob, cheat and deceive,
in spiteful honor among thieves,
our fortune is ill gotten gains,
skulls and crossbones mark our remains!

Argh!

Rose O.D.

I bring you a rose, as it blossoms from my love,
spreading petals toward the light,
touching far beyond the sight of land,
this flower's budding hand
presses its message to the heart,
while fragrant songs fill the air.
Exploding colors journey through our eyes,
to a universal recollection,
confession to the great connection,
in the ascension of this cosmic perfection,
to gain that blessed selection,
of God's attention. . .

Behold!
The Celestial Erection!

But it just looks like a rose to me.

Butts on Bicycles

Spinning wheels upon the heels of pumping legs,
leaning on the turns, diving down the hills,
and puffing up the next.

Rocking buns on swallowed seats,
bodies bent forth,
taking fists of wind upon the chin,
pressing on, toward clouds of speed
and grace on two-wheeled wings.

Finally, from one suspended drifting moment,
the spirit leaves the land and sails away,
rolling coitus on two wheels. . .

And when you find yourself back upon the road,
returning from that place words cannot describe,
on you go, down rolling highways,
through life's traffic,
pumping, humping, thumping,
on toward new fulfillment. . .
Speed dreaming through exotic lands,
whilst the Spirit's screaming,

"Look Ma, no hands!"

Diaspora Smack-Down

Again, all at once, that doleful refrain,
the bidding war for more,
potshot at a choice,
squandering the life force that we just ain't got,
on crackerjack pipedreams-one in each box!
Every four years it's all up for grabs!
Out of the woodwork, truth-sucking termites,
                                  level all in their path,
tilting transient tariffs taxing *what the traffic will bear,*
while working the crowds in delusional grandstands
                                  of swaying opinion.
Ninety-day wonders salute general platitudes,
turning backroom deals with unshackled shysters,
fake undivided dividend interests, in a two-Ponzi system,
parting fools from their cause,
serving two masters, with distraction and sham,
debates on the poles, *de' fish' on de' fire,*
seasoned with bombast, and dragged through the mire;
adding substance-less substance, to our tasteless desire.
Voter extortion confidently pedaling influence,
equivocating dollars with good sense,
                                  trading trinkets for values.
Like we forgot our geography.
They can't do it without us!

Mushrooming problems: too dangerous to ignore,
too expensive to overhaul,
just like Rome, comes before the great fall,
the world's here to remind us, "gravity sucks!"

Does different mean better?

We unite for a reason, all else would be treason.
For once and for all,
am I my brother's keeper?
Some brothers are sisters.
There is truth to be answered!
Whose word is a bond?
Don't trade it for bondage.
Deny what you will... Will you?
Won't you? Do you? Don't you?
What's in your wallet?

What?

What's your type? Hype? Gripe?
What's your sign? Line? Kind? Design?
Leaning? Meaning? Problem? Issue?
Addiction? Conviction? Dereliction? Friction?
Question? Suggestion? Regression?
Reference? Preference? Deference?
Name? Claim? Fame? 10/20?
Secret? Intent? Regret?
Dream? Or, scheme?
Do you want to scream?
Contention? Retention? Convention?
Fear, near, or dear;
i.e., what have you been smoking?

The Dying of the Light
& The Year of Promised Fright

A natal tale from the cradle's travail:
Winter Solstice 17;
an austere Capricornian sun on ice,
zero degrees,
rising house, moon,
Virgo dipped twice,
squared Sun to the Fourth,
afflicted, homeless and aged,
this peckish chart tune,
sung by a loon.

Jumpin' Jupiter, second house Libra,
imbalanced spend-thrifting,
USDA inspected, subjected,
infected, highly protected and suspected. . .

The third house, where nobody's there,
Scorpio's drive-by curdles the scare.

The Fourth house is haunted by
broken Sagittarian promises.
Mercury's gagged, bound at the door,
while Saturn condemns the Sun's
"Home for the Poor."

More Capricorn baggage sits in the Fifth.
Pluto hired Gloria Allred for a Venus defiled,
objectified and denied,
The case will be tried!
The guilty crucified.

A riot broke out in Aquarius
Cell Block Six.
Mars squares water and wind
to fortify hurricane force,
dealing pharmaceuticals and "horse."

Cellmate Neptune, can't stand the pain,
the same old refrain.
Recovery and healthcare
are still on their own,
what the traffic can bear,
blasts into the unknown.

Seventh House Pisces partners turn on a dime,
so soon they will,
just give them the time.
Chiron stands vigil over the grief,
with its renown for band-aid relief.

The door was left open at Aries' Eighth House!
Uranus barged in and killed the Door Mouse.
He ate all the porridge, slept in the beds,
broke all the chairs, and burnt the house down,
in excessively natural acts of rebellion.
And that made the Earth mad as one Hellion.

The Ninth House in Taurus is slated for remodel,
Pluto's still groping Venus,
so nothing's happening, full throttle.

Tenth House Gemini's reputation
hangs Midheaven high.
If you wonder what's going on,
fake news tells you why,
"Mercury's gagged, retrograde, opposition arrest."
Remember this answer, it'll be on the test.

Stop by Eleventh House Cancer,
who'll commiserate your tears,
then you get to listen,
when she tells you her fears.

We can just guess what happened
to Leo's Twelfth House.
Destined to decline, kicked in the Node,
eclipsed by a shadow, and its power erodes;
the Sun's home in the Fourth was invaded,
ransomed to the hilt,
just like Puerto Rico,
the whole place must be rebuilt.

The culprit:
Guardian Trustee, Saturn,
started it all,
destroying trust and tradition,
now he's building a wall!

A Dish for the Gods

One on one, cheek to cheek,
mano-a-mano, body to body,
desperately clamoring to become
vaporous melting minds, spirits,
and libidos with meat dripping cheese,
in aroused reaction to the law of attraction,
blending orgasmically in the pizza of love.

I spread open your box
inhaling your pheromonal aroma.
Kissing your pepperonis, supple and soft,
sucking sweet cheese delights,
through tender caressing bites.
The mouth-watering scent of anchovies,
willingly tickles my salacious appetite.

My senses peak in erectness,
as I lustfully devour the heavenly hour
of gorging this flower of grace.
Unified, perfectly timed and well-spaced,
I orgify cosmic pie,
in the nirvanic capture of rapture,
planting my face in place,
to become one on fire
with the emotional ocean of desire.

Smoke 'Em If You've Got 'Em

Beached Balls, Hallowed Halls, Street-fight Calls,
Tempered Squalls, Pincushion Dolls,
Taken Falls, Closing Walls, Regressing Crawls,
Unwarranted Galls, Perfect Flaws.

Tasted Rage, Flaunted Scorn,
Deliverance assured through trapdoor cures,
betwixt reality, and darkness.

Here's mine.
Where's yours?

Smoke 'em if you've got 'em.

What's mine is yours to try,

Here. . .
Breathe deep. . .

Some forbidden fruits,
tasted by dream-crazed historicadores. . .

what's in your pipe?

your eyes betray your words

your eyes betray your words,
darting to avoid response,
lips conceal secret longings,
to revive faint scents and flavors
that tarry in regard,

uneasy closeness
stampedes the senses,

hearts rush to judgment. . .

Intuitively parting
guarded sorrows
and intent. . .

Passing
painfully
into

unfamiliar worlds,
numbness,
and
despair. . .

        As you leave,

        nuance
        festers in abandon

        to seek

        unknown

              alone. . .

I Told You So!

Our stomachs are growling,
the old man's scowlin',
like we're givin' 'im gas!

He thinks he's runnin' the show, screamin',
"Kiss my ass!"

We're livin' it up,
like fossil fuel fools,
while we ravage our resources,
and dissolve all the rules.

Dig through refuse
to find our next meal.
We trust in our leaders
and, "The art of the deal!"

But, they're in the death-throws of consumption,
seductively swayed by the narcistical gumption
of one red-tied devil,
who won't say what he means,

while we bloat up with toxins,
as the vultures cruise our scene.

Cockroaches and rats re-zone the hood,
past depraved, fallen virtues,
where greatness once stood.

Famine-plagued blood-suckers drive us insane,
as roving death squads make US great again.

We're a nation of addicts in lifestyle withdrawal,
three-time repeat offenders of humanity's betrayal.

Hand-picked inquisitional injustice
of incompetent domain,
cast final judgment, guilt, shame, and pain.

Go about your business, take your last rites.

Leave your freedom unguarded,
                        give up, die, or fight.

I told you so!
There's no place to go!
No place to stay!
We're all going to pay!

Throwaway children choke on their cries!
We whore the world and all of its lies!
Vanity owns the pimp who hides the truth!
He gives you a kiss for speaking sooth!

What care you of a snuffed-out lamp,
as long as your style doesn't cramp?

Are you the one,
        and they're the rest?
When it's them,
        are you impressed?

Someone, or thing,
would rip us off!

But still we're robbed,
        and still we scoff
                at what we know is true.

While the game is played,
        they've made a slave 'a you.

Buy their oil, burn your lamp.
You get burned, your style gets cramped.

Eat the garbage
      they sell as food.

You'll eat each other
      when they're in the mood.

"Who are they?!"
      The cry will swell.

Whoever they are,
         they'll never tell. . .

They'll rule men's lives,
   make 'em limp and run,
      for fun and profit,
         with knives and guns.

And you and me,
we'll live in fear,

afraid to lose

what lives made so dear.
         One question lingers
            when we slit our own throats.

         "What was valued so little
            when we cast our votes?"

Big House Blues

I got blown away in Texas,
and didn't catch the gaposis of the Sneaky-Pete,
'til someone caught me doing it out back.
One more bust, and I'm set to howl.
This hot shot Charlie's got one more dogfight!
Get back! House Harry's cruisin' through. . .
"How do you do?!"
And the wigs are flipped, it's pig-shaved jarhead slick!
Piffed and piffed again,
and the AA don't want the action, too many burns.
Roll your own, stroke a bone, the seed is thrown,
                                       lie there an' groan;
Just a load 'a wind shakin' the air.
Purple loco fries the mind;
here comes Jerk McGee, geek first class,
let 'im pass…
The perfect crime is robbing time, to blow it on your dreams.
Cover the door! Kiss the floor!
God, I hate being poor!
Toot the ringer! The grab joint's clear!
The heist is on!
Loot the cash! Make the stash! It's almost dawn!
Cool your rod!
Split the catch outside town! Hug the ground!
Don't get found slinkin' round!
Sheeeiittt! Got tracked down!!!
Frame-up time! The jip is on!
Can't trust nobody no more!
Gone bust, talkin' turkey with the wrong Clem!
Mugshot Sherman and the keys are turnin'
three to five, take 'a dive!
And I'm still alive,
and scratchin' on this Texas wall;
and I wanna go home…

Dancing

I dance for life, I dance forever
when I stop, it's over forever.

I dance to survive, I dance for meaning,
I dance to keep the world twirling,
when the music stops, never is forever.

I dance for birth, I dance for death,
when I stop, tomorrow flies away.

I dance for love, I dance for compassion,
when I stop, I lose all feeling.

I dance for you, I dance for me,
when I stop, I will be lost,
and all will dance on by,
leaving emptiness in its shadow.

I dance forever,
the universe keeps rhythm,
in our time;

we all dance every season
for every reason.

Dance!

Dance with me,

. . .and all will be. . .

Dancing. . .

Amber Sound Flow Freely

Amber sounds flow freely
teasing
darting
caressing
stony caverns in my mind.
Whishing colors
grow from shadows
reaching in,
soothing, stroking,
pricking, cutting!
Stabbing, slashing!!
Blinding, screaming!!!
Deafening, crippling!!!!
Mmmm…
Mmmmmm!
Mmmmmmmm!!!

Love those day-old flashes!

Get What You Need

How many wayfarers pass by
on great horse-muscled engines
of might,
or will,
or doubt of the natural laws,
defiant young near-siters of balancing hues,
rolling hope chests of virtues as long as an arm
stretched 'round the good things in life?
Keep off!
Don't shoot!
No one's loaded!
And so am I!
Now
I think I'll cry
before I die,
and laugh,
and split in half
the haul of knowing all.

Secret weapons
don't help the odds
on running out of spaces in the ground.

Don't drop the ball and have to crawl back home
again!

It's time for a shrewdness in loving it!
You know!
That life you lead
where
what you need
you always get

Then walk on down the road,
and score some more!

And say your prayers
and thank some more,
you know what for!

It's back to that!

Don't be the fool;
you're still the tool!

Use your style when you call your shots,
and in a while

you will have thought your way from here to there,
and no one will care
but you,

because
you stopped to plant the seed
like someone did before

and it will fill the needs
it needs to fill
for more to score
and plant again.

We always get what we need.

Now

there is no need

to say any more...

Red Rover, Red Rover,
Let October Be Over

Occupy!!!
What the Guy Fawkes?!
No room, in a twerking economy!
The bomb's still a threat! 99% terminal nostalgia.
1% pure purchasing profit power of doom.
"Those were the days!"
"Move on!" they exclaimed in a glaze,
as they're carted away.

Who am us, anyway?
Counting ciphers, phantom temps, sweat-shoppers,
                                      inside-out the box,
Foreclosure disclosures, conviction evictions?!
Still thinking? Like that?!

History's being rewritten; electronically enhanced,
new suits in tight pants.
Tricked by a tweet! Picked by a nose!
Hysterical figures, sound-biting their woes.

Seasonal déjà-vu:
nuclear winters chem-trailing the food chain,
melting our ice cream and the bears in white PJs,
in the green-house rush for black gold.
Greed never gets old.
FEMA financed, for famine and fun.
Toxic planet proliferation equivocation!
Global warming is swarming!
That's what we're talking about!
And talking, and talking, and talking. . .

Immigration Reform! Insecurity Checkpoints!
More human rights! Wrong!
Mutant brothers from alien mothers,
speaking in tongues, encrypting our meaning,
like headlights and deer; take it to the wall!

Where all the "ayes" had it,
poised and locked in the crosshairs
of the Death Valley daze;
Congress is more than adjourned.
If you can't handle the truth, use tongs!

Can we tether this weathered political climate,
                                      gone out of control?"
Coming soon, to a local straw poll near you!

Just like Halloween... Every day for a year... Then again...
Candy-ass traditions, for a toothless economy;
bank on it! Again, and again...

Perfectly pert pink pumpkins,
in "D" cup demise... For the cure...
Fantasy football lingerie, business as usual,
burning hot bras, hapless and strapless,
every year, for the cure...

Still, looking for jobs is harder than work.
Minimum wages for maximum profits,
suffering *Plantation Facistitist*,
'til it jumps up to bite us!

Prescribing pharmaceutical futures all across our nation,
ain't no refunds on life's cancellation,
juxtapose that jocose, bellicose, overdose with reservation.

Give me a break; everyone's on the take!
What else can we fake?!
If we stand for commitment, they'll have us committed!
If we blink, then, we sink.

Oh well,
Someday... Never comes...

Haven't we seen enough, already?
Again?

Nickle-Bag Reality

Time ran rabid in passion's front room
while alligator clips sealed our fate.
Don't smile happy tonight,
you johnnie-cake fake,
I'll deal with you when I'm straight!

And clock's whiskers twitch and itch,
playing youth's exorcist,
that ticking sweet fairy elf witch…

"Hail to thee, Queen Slipstitch!
What's the pitch?

Please, please!
Don't pinch my plainly sanely brain!

Time is just an endless train,
leading from our verses to refrains!"

It's got to stop!!!
Cut the power, throw the switch!!!

But you never stop ticking, do you, you son-of-a-bitch!

Jizz What You Want

You've got me right where you want me, tethered and bound,
and in my excitement, you reveal my renown,
erect glistening stiffness, in rigid heavenward bliss,
awaiting the touch of your life sucking kiss.
Stripped naked and dripping,
you take me in hand,
in the grip of excitement,
my prowess grows grand.
Rocket throbbing ready.
You kiss it for luck,
and your lips are so graced;
sweet guardians of the most heavenly place.
With no second thought, you swallow it whole.
Deep down, it goes,
well passed your voice box,
and your cute double chin.
It makes your neck swell,
to twice normal size.
On it keeps going,
to your tummy and thighs.
It then makes your toes curl
as it hits bottom and stops.
"A little further," I groan.
And then your jaw drops.

The Saga of Brother Rat

Invocation

Mongrel faces forge night from light.
Through bloodstained lifeless haunts,
soft echoes free-fall hard,
from ageless terrors, dead with rot.
Hoof beats crack frozen blindness.
From a distant corridor comes the call,
on he draws to kinsmen all!

Crashing through discarded skulls, and passing on,
Brother Rat descends to hell,
upon a fire-forged unicorn!
Through open gates he passes
by twisted sentry, with matchlock poised.

"Where be mother flame?" he drools.
"Beyond and beyond!" shrieked him back.

The Rat spit blood, and laid haste his reins
through a cloud of pain.
Down, down, into the bowels of greed,
the flames scorched black upon his mask.
Quicklime tortures ravage fears,
as eternal darkness fades into years.

His strength renewed, he parts the womb,
in search of new torments, to feed upon emptiness.
Across a universe of spinney darkness,
seeking blood-knotted comrade, and fellow rat,
and through a trapdoor spies hazy gray on hazy black.
"Squint Wretch! A meal! Gawk again!"
"Aye; forsaken and denied! There be thou,
whom Brother Rat shall cause to end!"

Eulogy

You play your virtual football,
you've broken number four.
Mr. Toad slays Mr. Mole,
and the law is at your door.
It matters not who you fear.
Compassion is a stranger here.

A three-legged dog stops to die,
slime is only sold in pints,
you're drowning in your liquid lies,
death's shadow has a blood-red tint.
"Who cares? Have another beer!"
Compassion is a stranger here!

You raped your daughter yesterday.
So, what was left for her to say?
The question: "What to do today,
on this, the holiest of days?"
"Kill the dog, he's acting queer!"
Compassion is a stranger here!

Snake-eyes show you've lost your race.
Crush the blind man as he crawls.
Hatred has carved your swollen face.
Your homemade hell contains no walls!
Satan's voice is sounding clear.
"Compassion is a stranger here!"

You'll soon die and decay one dark night,
and take with you a world of sin,
and someone will open your window nailed tight,
to let the fresh sweet air in;
and a warning sign shall be posted near,
"Compassion was a stranger here."

Benediction

My peace I give to you,
my peace I leave with you.
And Mercury sighs a poem,
the silver oracle of love,
to pierce the heart of life,
within the heart of God.

And one candle burns in the night!
Hope?
Yes, hope,
for the living,
for the dead,
for the loved,
for the unloved,
and in one last desperation,
hope for us. . .

What Is Change?

Haven't we learned,
anything?

What is change,
without resolve?

Cell Phone Eavesdropping

"I got really lucky,
I was in an accident,

And it wasn't my fault.
Even though, they said it was,

they couldn't prove it!
It's the manufacturer's fault!
They know it was!

I went to stop, and nothing happened;
my leg was numb!

The brakes went out!

I just rear-ended somebody right into the next life. . .

I'm afraid to take it back on the freeway,
'cuz,
they just said the brakes are OK. . .

I just don't want to get into another accident.

My leg's been gettin' numb lately; twice today!

When I had the accident,
I had to get out, and walk it off!

You want me to pick you up?

I'll do it, as long as I don't have to go on the freeway. . .

If something happens to that car,
I'll never be able to prove it wasn't my fault!"

Auld Lang Synge
(Old Long Ago)
>to R<small>ALPH</small> "B<small>ONZO</small>" S<small>TEADMAN</small>

Another millennium ends,
it's time to sacrifice the virgin to the pagan gods.
Are there any left? Virgins?
No, gods!
Don't cut the cord! Not yet!
Laundry first! We want to look as good as we could!
Never was there such a day of predictable uncertainty.
The moon appears, we're on our own.
We saw the U.F.O., and there we go!
Predictable uncertainty,
like waking in the night, stirred by a presence,
that should not be, but is,
and we bear witness
to the darkness of our own enlightenment,
a familiar place, no stranger than
the back of our hand.
We meet again, in that moment of clarity,
and the fear we thought we all forgot returns,
calling our name.
We respond involuntarily compliant.
We want to go, but are afraid of what we're most assured,
a familiar journey, destination unknown.
Left behind, left for dead,
left and buried in our head.
Compelling, fading recollection. . .
Let it be. . .
Let it go. . .

We were here, then we're gone,
we were many, then we're none.
We stand alone in our togetherness,
and await the great beyond. . .

Boneroo Wood

I am of ancient celestial dust
spawned from one manic act.
Launched into a universe
of delightfully creamy abstract.

There's a tree grows in my forest,
'sprung straight up one special night.
Those who explore and behold it,
are stricken by awesome fright.

It juts ever upward to a pandering sky,
where the well-hung fuzzy nuts belie,
as hazards to high flyers,
and inspiration for mile-highers.

Suicidal zealots slide up its well-worn trunk
and perch upon its mushroom top,
where they writhe and sway in swinging funk
to the mantra of, "Oh please, don't let it stop!"

Then comes a climax thundering huge.
Nature's payload throbs, jolts, and cuts lose,
To erupt and spew a gushing deluge,
that soaks the universe in sweet sticky juice.

Kiss Another One Good-Bye

I'm staring at the hills from the bordello,
wonderin' when they're comin' down,
wonderin' when this house is gonna change around me.

What, me change?
No, I'll change the hills first,
paint another house red,
and charge at the door.

My soul is shakin' at the foundation,
as I kiss another one good-bye
changin' all the way. . .

Will it change, ever?
Did it ever?
Can it ever?
Never ever?

Hey, what am I doing here?
I could be out changing things. . .

Or,
did I change my mind?

Hunni-Do Fixes the World!

Every time I hear those calls for help!
"Honey!" "Baby!" "Daddy!" "Dear!"
Or, the plaintive cry of a baby.
I jump into my Big-Boy cargo pants,
with emergency flare utility belt,
to answer the shrieks of distress!
I just can't help it.
I want to make things *All Right!*
If there's any question,
I want to find the answer,
cure or remedy.
I want to fix it!
Be there to comfort, heal,
or stand in the gap.
No job to tough,
no problem too petty,
to make the world
safer, saner, nicer, happier,
less crappier, more perfect!
How can I be so predictable,
and programmable,
still dare to care who stepped in poo?
Ah, for the life of a sucker!
That's how I feel.
What a schlemiel!
What kind of a deal is that?
Husbandry the world!
I'm hard wired that way.
It's not a question of macho duty,
more a desire to stifle the whining.
But it never stays fixed very long.
What else can I do, fix, repair, or improve?
Maybe Stupid-Hero is my calling.
Yeah, it's kinda nice to feel needed. . .

All That Fuss

You're still here!
And so am I!

To the end of our wits
and back again!

Every time it gets tough
and panic sets in,
the heart starts racin'
muscles tighten,
the mind goes blank,
we get frightened!

Two weeks later
we're still alive.
We take a deep breath
of wonder
that we survived!

How did all that work out?!

Just when we thought
we had the route!
We lost our courage,
not knowing what to do!

Eventually…
Wishes do come true!

What's in your closet?

Clothes?

Maybe we should change. . .

Godsending Gerunding

Lay, lie,
sit, sigh,
crawl, try,
stand, vie,
run, fly,
do, die,
fade, cry,
end, hie!

Laying, lying,
sitting, sighing,
crawling, trying,
standing, vying,
running, flying,
doing, dying,
fading, crying,
ending, hying!

Never Will Be Forever

Vanity wilts in a half-heart attempt
to conceal the pain
revealed by the tracks
that lead here and back;
self-exile in remission,
by faint omission.

Empty shadows still remain
in this ballad with one refrain,

nowhere again,

only pain

take a ride,
to "end of the line,"
just short of "no return"

walk it back…

a good cry
needs no reply,

lost in recollection,
open heart rejection,

all becomes unwound,
a heart falls off the merry-go-round;

time will nod its head,
and make your bed
an empty stead,
as it clicks a final stroke.

Not one word spoken
silence slumps unbroken,

never to resist,
when being kissed,
or feel so blessed
in deep caress.

We're born
to cry
when love dies.

Nothing confirms what was

deficient blessings forget the way

damaged hearts dissolve
in vaporous denial

a bell keens for thee and me…

"Hello?"
"I love you!"
"One more minute!"
"A glancing gasp!"

"Please!!!"

Dust dry darkness drains the dream

"Goodbye…"

The wind won't care, we will go
and blow what was, to winter snow…
someday, wounds may not show,
eternity will forget…

then…
we know
                       never will be forever…

Reading the Seeds

Through serious consequences
our vehicle's thrown.
Lost on an outbound planet,
destination unknown.

Conscious decisions dissolve
as the solar winds roar
'cross castaway wreckage,
floating abandoned evermore.

Past posted warnings of what came before.
All access is blocked by a giant cosmic locked door.

That neglected detail, the key, began this demise,
rotting all thoughts deemed prudent and wise.

Subliminal seduction sways every soul,
and taints all perceptions of attainable goals.

Responses runs rampant
throughout the land
placing fingers on triggers
and swords in our hands.

Taking heed of the seeds of our needs,
hurled into the oblivion
of our mindless deeds,
infecting every surrogate word or prayer.
Repent and resolve,
that key is the seed, in truth dedication,
to free all to evolve creations' new nation…

A Fine-Tuned Machine

We trusted the man with our power,
He squanders our wealth by the hour.
We trusted him to do what's best;
On empty promises he screams, "We must invest!"
He needs good help; you might get hired!
Become a brown nose, or else you're fired!
His plan's so secret he doesn't know.
Disagree with him, you'll have to go!

You can make America great!
Just don't get snookered, when he switches the bait!

The Seven Veils of Crisis

The double-crossed virtues,
dressed in a bigot's lament,
bleed like a stuck pig,
in righteous looks of contempt.

"We've slain the last demon!"
A creation misused,
on time-temporal neglected,
the devil-bomb fused.

Free willing and truth-less,
and fruitless, and toothless,
and dead on the ground,
groping for answers,
and nothing is found.

On cross-legged oxen,
they march to the sun,
with dung crowned scarabs
in brigades of twelve deep,
while the pious lie weary,
and cloaked in a sleep.

Hyenas and jackals bay at their heels,
and into the cities roll the great wheels,
through despair and dejection,
and the silence of guilt,
out of fear and oppression,
a great dunghill is built.

Limbo fantasy madness!
A new monster arrived!
Build it bigger and greater,
and more dug was contrived.

The sun fell from glory,
dung blocked out its face.
In one simple maneuver
the world laid in waste.

And the dung lords and tribunes
worshipped the dung,
and the fashion of dungdom
was in the dung that one flung.

Those pillars of virtue,
the beacons of light,
succumbed to the darkness,
sinking deep out of sight.

Behold!

Every dung-brain was stricken,
lack-luster of wit!
And all, they did vanish,
to drown in their own shit.

`O Behave, or Not OB

Obadiah's obbligato mandates obedient obeisance.
Oberon the obese obediently
utters muttering the obiter dictum obituary objectively,
objectifying the objet d'art and objet d' trouve' of subterfuge
to the objurgation oblation of the few;
obligating every first and third persons
the onus as obligee onto the reluctant obligor
of obliquity,
obliterating import into oblivion
obnoxiously obnubilating reality,
and the middleman,
obscenely,
obfuscating
obvious
obscurity.

Obsequious observations
obsess compulsively,
over obsolete obstacle courses
of obstinate wanabe obstetricians
obstreperously obstructing
the insurmountable,
obtaining
obtruding
obtrusive
obturations
obtusively
obsessively
obtunding
and obverse,
sans obviation.

Obviously!

No Twix, Santa's Tweet

Santa knows what you want.
Can you guess what you'll get?
If I may be so blunt,
there is no secret.

Are you worthy of praise?
Do you sleep well at night?
After those naughty ol' days,
when you scream, yell and fight?

Are you on Santa's nice list?
Did you make someone cry?
You get the gist,
so, ask yourself, "Why?"

You can be such an angel,
and treat everyone nice.
Mind your good sense and teachers,
'cuz I check my list twice.

When I'm in your hood,
I'll stop by your place,
and I'll know you've been good,
by the look on your face.

I'm watching you daily,
I know what you do.
When you give love and respect,
it comes back to you.

Happy Holidays!

This Party Sucks!

This party sucks! There's nothing to do!
Then all at once, I caught sight of you.
For this I'd pay penance, or even redeem.
And there you stood, in a sleep-walking dream,
a foreshadowing glance,
I might have a chance,
to surrender what could be,
imagined, or not;
peaking my interests!
Now, it's hard,
to maintain,
anonymity,
and not seem on guard.
You've made me your soldier,
attention stiff, and erect.
If you examined me closer,
you'd begin to suspect,
I'm armed and dangerous,
and bang at your gate.
In rigid compliance,
I march to my fate.
Hypnotized,
as I gaze in your eyes,
lashed to my mainmast,
to the siren's demise.
A glancing pass at your island,
I stumble my strut.
"Excuse me!" you swelter,
"Did you touch my butt?"

A Pilgrimage of Love

In search of purest love.
Unattainable perfection
consecrated bonds of grateful touch.
Wayfarers halt mid-prayer
smitten in that moment of encounter,
staring back, in one fixed determined gaze
skies dazzle within your eyes,
to harmonize lyrical allure.
Nectar sweetness flavors crisp air,
enticed to revelation;
overwhelmed by aromatic presence,
permeating every motive and desire,
blushing sensations to an overload
of transcending euphoria,
beyond all caress of understanding.
Reason loses logic…
Love responds in acute surrender

Recovering from Life

America, It's your fault!
I am addicted to a sense of well-being,
knock on wood, if I could, or should, need to or not!
Whole truth or half; don't make me laugh! Ha, ha.
Desire me to introduce you,
my darling, dearest, damnedest, digression.
There's no truth to it; if you read my meaning.
Losers get found, arrested and bound.
Paving the path with good intentions, slightly ever,
                                            almost never,
free-feeling and fat, down on the mat, dumb-struck I sat.
Just like that! Don't kick that cat!
Keep walkin' the wire, high on desire.
'Got stuck in the mire,
crossin' this great nation of, *-ation;*
nationalize-ation, automize-ation, rationalize-ation,
victimize-ation, globalize-ation,
devaluize-ation;
we've changed the station and cancelled vacation!
Don't touch that dial! Cut to denial!
You haven't the time to make an excuse,
as behaviors run lose.
But, you're between friends;
a veritable pip-squeak amongst mystics!
Allow me to compromise your demise,
sucker-punch your reputation; it's looking quite flat;
let's pump you up; that's where it's at!
Look under your hood! Ooh! That ain't lookin' so good.
Ah-ha! It's tune-up time! The concert begins!
Me-me-me! You-you-you! No, not you! Me-me-me!
Forget you! It's all about me!
What am I saying? Ah, forget about it! What was I talking about?
It doesn't matter!
Can I have more?
One portion distortion?
That's better...Aaahhh!

Earthbound Astrologers

Earthbound astrologers, you know who you are:
Aries, you ram butt you head 'gainst your good sense,
Taurus, bull-fling and trash all that you have,
Gemini, twins tweaking out loud, confirming two is a crowd,
Cancer, crab mooder, side-stepping baggage-bound brooder,
Leo, lion denying the Narcistical truth,
Virgo, virginal analyst, purity processified, never satisfied,
Libra, scales tipping and tripping opinions, imbalanced at best,
Scorpio, scorpion, snapping its claws,
              an overkill stinger betrays its own cause,
Sagittarian, horse-assed archer, never true to the mark,
Capricorn, goat with a fish tale, no one believes,
Aquarius, water bearer of toxic intentions, tainter of tides,
Pisces, fish off the hook, unschooled and forsook.
If that is your nature, and that's all you will be,
keep it under a rock, that's where you'll find me.

Intellectual Suicide

Note to self:
Stand up and speak from the heart,
lay it out to the universe
in eight billion lifetimes or less!
It's not our first cosmic rodeo,
ropin' the golden calf,
bustin' the bronc,
ridin' the bull,
speakin' the heart,
stackin' the verse,
feelin' the pull
of the power of seduction,
goin' to far
so close to the hour
lacking the recall
of a mindless bodiless soul.
Principles undone,
losing it all
without any fanfare
lost in the great mall.

In an instant of clarity
our eyes meet
confirming disparity.

Judgment becomes final,
ideals on trial
in single-file quick lime
sunset denial.
Words said and heard,
meanings are blurred,
set on the shelf,
fell on the floor,
left on the table.
Don't answer the door!

Decisions deferred,
points lost and forgot.
He who spoke to his purpose
was left in the haze of the maze.

Those with agendas
decry, "Suicide!"
"It makes no sense,
rhyme or reason,
so out of season!"

I cast pearls before swine,
then get in line
as they root through my pockets,
strip riches from sockets,
pigeon-holing,
discounting, controlling
every facet of power,
installing guilt, fear, and shame
as tools to keep fools
in their place.

It's Intellectual Suicide
to step up and speak,
like some kind of freak;
a poet in purgatory
who reminds fellow travelers,
they've been marooned;
urging action to words
in attempts to combat
bully brigades,
of insurmountable odds,
that come face to face,
with an absentee god;
whom I represent
as collateral baggage,
and equilateral mackerels,
friends to the trout,
divining the route,

knowing full well
truth will rat itself out,
compromising extremes,
expelling all doubts.

"Death by consensus,
torture by text;
closure through censure,
and the power
of redemptive deception."

God and I
know the answer.

Turn on the light!

There is no secret!

I must be as stupid
as you think,

to think that you
care what I think.

Socrates lives!

Wait Station Earth

We walk in like a bunch of virgins, looking for assurances,
while everyone sits and stares, waiting for the word.
We know something's going to happen,
and it does,
and nobody likes it.
So, we twitch and twitter induced distractions,
simulating sorry moments, as they melt into days,
squeezing every second out of life,
stacking them by the weeks,
as they bleed into months, years, and centuries
assuming habitual traditions shrouded by the fog of faith.

Depression overwhelms all reason.
Alone, once again.
We played a pawn in someone else's game,
and whimper, "rip off", all the way home.
If we could only find the door!
And no one comes or goes…

Sit and sigh, and wonder why,
                hope and promise wilt and die…
Give a dog-eared excuse for not knowing your part,
stuff your pockets with the virtues of a dreamland fancy,
leaking all the bubbles
                from that graven image of your purpose.

What bothers you, bothers everyone.
That same foolishness that overwhelms us all.
The will to live and hope for something better,
something more than what we have;
it's the only thing that keeps us going down the path,
into that land of being what we think we should,
passing through a sea of strangers,
beyond the dazzling warning lights of planned obsolescence,
to that epiphany: that we'll remember when we get there,
and leaving,
never know again. . .

Mercutio, King of Cats

*This is an homage to a sequel to **Romeo and Juliet** by William Shakespeare. Written by Crystophver R, first as a stage play, it became an award-winning screenplay. When characters exit in Shakespeare's play, they enter in Mercutio, King of Cats. Unlike the tale to two star-crossed lovers, this is the tale of two star-crossed brothers.*

Heir apparent to a high-jacked dream
one orphaned wayfarer, saved by a lion
falls sacrificial victim to his own charm.
Marooned on a Silk Road mirage.
Riding the masthead to the deep,
blessed by the curse of Cathay,
charted by Marco Polo's obsession,
beguiling the reaper his due.

Renounced and forgotten by familial ruin,
a back-streets royal cryptic alliance.
Comes a young street lion survivor conniver
in search of careless attentions,
to stalk, sniff out, and plunder each corner, and niche.

Beyond the stench of the con
he manifests patchwork dreamscapes,
of memories that never were,
accented by the swash of a wicked slash,
as he exacts and levies
a tax on opium dreams.
Puffed-up and choking on arrogance,
two twinkling eyes, and a devout pledge
to die or get by, on words and his sword.

Grandiose promises to a lady of quicksilver,
fitting his passions to fashion,
squandering each precious moment,
to the flashpoint of death.

Wealth, station and cunning
ever the drive
conspiring to steal back

a life and his pride,
re-balance accounts,
disregard of the law
and the refrain of domain

at the risk of his own soul;
the weight of his heart,
'gainst the feather of truth.
 It's writ in the scroll!

Action and consequences
chart a course doomed to fail
plans unforeseen or expected
cause deadly travail.
Wounded in combat,
the lame King of Cats,
to reckon unscheduled sojourn
to the next life,

joined by his star-crossed brother,
led by the opium den Fairy Midwife,
to arrive at a limbo Bardo terrain.
She points them the way
to vanish,

two cats abandoned to stray,
revived and cursed in vexation,
to relive missing moments,
that masque hidden fears,
until all comes clear,
to balance the caveat,
befits a true King of Cats...

No Leg to Stand On

So you didn't vote!
You're a goner!
Like a virgin in Tijuana
hauling your junk
like a pack mule;
better an ass
than a fool!

Einstein's theory
on insanity:
shakin' the earth more than twice,
go on, roll the dice,
if your trigger finger's itchin',
it must be lice!

Like chasing your tail
in the dark,
now it's on video,
someone called you a narc.

Pip-pip, cheerio,
heard it on the radio!
Stiff-upper-lip,
don't get caught in your zip!
And all that sort of rot!

The world has gone to pot!

More Disney-Dow-delirium,
on the slaughterhouse floor
in a millennium continuum;
ask any stock market whore.

Better keep your Magic Kingdom Pass.

The happiest place on earth
ain't as funny as the funny money.

There's a new blockbuster coming
calculated to scare you into submission.
Listen!
You can hear the machinery humming;
full of special effects, like nuclear fission.

Give us a big heartfelt "Moo!"
you overfed piece 'a meat!
Downgraded from prime,
there's no choice.

It's in the bag,
you've lost your voice.

We'll all be the extras,
of biblical proportions,
making final installment assaults
as two-bit pure-bred juggernauts.

Playing the roles of questing pilgrims
as they morph into type-cast victims:
purse grabber,
gift gabber,
kid nabber,
secret blabber,
work scabber,
re-haber,
back stabber!

Get away from that mirror!
It's just the reflection
that leads to further infection!

Go on, sell off the land! (It's contaminated anyway)
Then move to Mars
and raise Avatars;
go ride around in a driverless hearse.
Life could be worse.

Solipsist-Station

You've been marginalized!
You know...by default,
that long, low rumbling sound... you know...
Social emotional security, developmentally challenged,
cultured by civilization, coddled by neglect,
prevarication equivocated, predilection by proxy,
election by abstention, and the majority of me!
Solipsists unite!
Ha-ha!
You're not here!
Surprise!
I penciled you in to illustrate my point.
Poof!
I drank the potion and became the ocean!
Here, fishy-fishy-fishy!
I'll grant your little wishy!
If you're tired of repeating yourself,
shut-up!
I've said enough!
Believe-you-me, they'll never believe you,
with your banal anal brainal retention invention!
One custom-made, hand-cancelled fantasy;
existence denied!!!

Are you still here?!
That's OK,
I know how to forget...

Bored Shortz

All right then!
All right now!
What to do?
Find that special place.
Ninety-seven ways to
occupy your space!

But here and now
we're havin' a cow!
Whoop-whoop-whoop-dee-wow!

It's time!
Do you do?
Or, do you don't?

Anything?
Or something?

Join the crowd!
Get on board!

Everyone's doing it!

Keep looking busy!

Avoid the inevitable!

Take your time;
just long enough
to forget about it.

Deep thought justifies boredom.

Think while you wait. . .

"It's All Right!"

It's the biggest no brainer in the history of mankind!
The greatest boon to boon-dogglers in the boon-docks, ever!
Me, I never could figure one jip from another.
If it ain't one thing, you got your druthers.
Don't just grin and bear it!
Try to tune-in and share it!
Someone chimes in "It's All Right!"
Without havin' to even stop,
and count your toes,
you count 'em anyway, just so you know,
they weren't lost in the shuffle
of life or limb.
You'll never really know, "It's all right!,"
if you just sit there, waitin' to be told.
Especially if you're old!
And, what do they know anyway?
They just say things to shut you up!

A Kiss

I beg a kiss,
    that touch of the surrender
        of shared secrets;
            confirmation of a momentary
    lifetime.

Two forces of temptation
        in defiance of a void
            constrained by the rationale of
    gravity.

Prevailed in reckless exploration,
    grafted to eternal wings
        of smoldering emotions,
            nurtured by the sweet warmth of
    desire,
            straining heavy at the details
    of a denial omitted;

indelibly encrypted
    with one imparted embrace,
        to extinguish and dissolve
            a million constellations,
                and one universe

that dwells somewhere forever…

The Earth Sucks

Here, at thirty-seven thousand light feet above tear level,

I've discovered a giant's-eye view of reality,

flexing its flabby mountains. . .

My vehicle grunts its declaration,

"The earth is only what it says it is,

A spinning sphere. . .

that brings up. . .

dow
      n"

Perfection Is What Is...

Perfection is what is...
    And life goes on...
        Until things change...
            Then...
                Perfection is what is...

Hallow Greetings

Welcome!
Addressed to the best, forget all the rest.
Embrace, then erase.
Recognize and despise,
nod and approved, with hat gesture removed,
to herald and to hail this intensive travail,
quite well received, sneered and deceived,
paying installment respects,
unsaid, and unseen!
Say what you mean!

AhhOhh!
Now, come secret taboos, habitual downgrades.
And, what do we say?
Programmed responses, like we don't even care!
"What's up!?" "What's comin' down!?" "What's going on?!"
"What's comin' off!? "What's happenin'!?"
"Hi!", maybe, "Hey!"
You can say nay to my "Hey!"
But, please don't bray like an ass!
Just let it pass, like the fumes, in the wash of your gas.
Do you dare to take care with the greetings you share?
Hello? Are you still there?

No wonder!
Offence should be totally taken!
Implied repliance activated; systems going gone:
more folly to wallow!

Like: "Why do you ask?" "Who wants to know?"
"Writing a book?" "It's the same as before!"
"Nothing has changed, not even my name!"
"The jury's still out!" "Don't make me shout!"
"Take a number!"

"Don't ask, and don't tell, we can't stand the smell!"

Uncool fellow fool... Use the right tool!
Fill in the blanks!
Attend tender salutations, give love in return,
uncork the kindness, ignore your own blindness,
like: "Salud,"
and "Aloha,"
going both ways...
Trendy!
Bipolar at best, close to the vest.

O well! Whatever!
I've got to go!

"Good-bye." "See you!" "Take care!" "Have a nice day!"
"Adios!" "Vaya con dios!" "Come back when you can stay!"

Again? Like that!?

Maybe we should start over with "Hi!" and "Bye!"
Why even try?

Never mind...

I can tell, I'm talkin' to the hand...

Back to "Business As Usual."

minding the store...
concern on ignore...
same as before...

Need I say more?

Malice of Forethought

Doing life for a victimless crime,
beyond vegan, beyond love,
everywhere footprints, grand handstands galore,
trying to live, without touching earth,
re-defined perfection,
time-base corrected,
triggered by the tsunami of pain,
and the joy of TMI,
stocked up in supply,
guaranteed revocable,
like fire and brimstone, it's smokeable;
new-laundered information,
uninformed, uniformity,
followed by keening and wailing,
"Don't mistake rewind for reset!"

Where are we going?
Where have you been, hunh?
Check your baggage,
let's bargain a plea,
negotiate a conviction,
there are so few left,
right?
You didn't do it . . .
Don't look at me.
Thank God for the fifth!
Want a slug? It goes down so easy.
Talk about life-altering experiences!
Life without pain is a world without rain;
loss of command with easy-fit waistband,
"Guilty as charged!" Livin' Triple-X Large!
Logic won't work in the land of the jerk.
Rationalize that!

The Rise and Fall of It All

What's going on, what's coming off?!
Yes, maybe no. . .
But, I'm not going to tell you. You know why?
Done there, been that, everything, everywhere!
See your way clear to join me in song,
a catchy little tune, you'll carry life-long.
You know the words, don't act like you don't,
quit wastin' time, hum what you will, or you won't.
You ain't foolin' no one!
Always ready to be elsewhere, anywhere but here.
And you are! Your mind just left the building,
leaving trashy excuses in your backwash regard,
huge carbon footprints throughout the yard.
Your mind ran away, and left your behind,
beyond all belief, in the deep depressions of community grief;
that familiar touch of the lonely one and only,
that holds us so close, and make us believers
                                       in what we fear most.
This is the nightmare we host coast to coast!
Shattering matters redeeming concern,
                              dumbing down all around,
separating hope from the spoils of our fears.
Underworld music echoes our moods, rancid pedal tone arias,
pandemic nocturnal death-songs,
cryptically whimper secret requiem prayers,
begging another chant at life and its strife.
Melting-pot masses of untreated squalor,
trickling down through the street-sleeping comatose,
slamming each dose with a lost sense of undoing;
hopelessly nestled in gutter-side mansions,
every profile on speed-dial,
forecasting what's gone and beyond.
And what do we do? What can we do? What will we do?
Words. . .That's what we do best.
Make deeds of our words. . .
How long has it been? How long will it take?

The Covenant of Light

The season is the reason that makes devotion our intent,
and in the spirit of fertile blindness,
we chance to share our love.
Born as strangers, star-crossed and destined, beyond account,
and in a twinkling, tantamount, foreshadowing one,
casting love where light forgot to show,
reading like the saga of forever,
through miraging deserts, and swelling valleys,
searching out new promise, to share and live.

Commitment is tomorrow's strength, and substance
filling willing hands of two young spirits,
who lift each other over often stumbled ground,
driven by forces far beyond perception.

We're beckoned here to witness, and share confessed secrets,
as they make their purpose known,
and in the instant of a lifetime
more understanding's thrown.

Come out into the sunlight, show the world love has no doubt;
go upon the mountain, let your essence shout!
Love is the most painful joy of all.
And we are joined together, in answer to this call
when the blossoms of desire fill the nose of reason,
announcing, the blessed advent of a new age and season.

We're born, we cry, learn to laugh, fall in love,
and if we're lucky, carry on, 'til we can't party anymore.
Here we are, future faces of the past,
gathered on this once and distant shore.

Confirm this covenant of love, as two speak as one,
to make the world take notice of what magic has been done.
Two living life, as if it were an art,
making all believers in sensations of the heart;
pumping, thumping valentines from God,
telling you he loves you more than there is light,
to fill a blind man's sight;
more than all the moonbeams can fill an empty night.

There's more love within us than creation ever knew,
a love for all the ages, a love of one for two,
and gently locked within, a love from me to you.

Go forth unto this universe with fruitful hearts of love,
and know this moment has been hallowed,
                            by the forces from above,
and let your light so shine, so all mankind shall know,
that from this sacred union a greater love shall grow,
and stand in living witness from this moment on,
to light the steps before you,
with the blessings of a new day dawned!

Zeugma in Action

Inanity
inbred,
incapably
indecent,
ineffectually
infeasible,
ingenuity
inharmoniously
iniquitous,
injuring
inklings
inly
inmost,
innately
inoperative
inpetto,
inquisitionally
inroading
insanity,
interminably
inutile,
invocative
inwardly
in-xenophobic
in-your-face
in zeugma!

zeugma: the use of a word to modify or govern two or more words, applying to each in a different sense, or making sense with only one.

Seeking Comfort

Closing eyes softly,
plush, fragrantly pleasing,
soothing, euphoric perfect peace.
Relaxed restful repose,
stretched-out
in relieved, poised well-being,
abundantly sufficient and gratified.
Luxuriously plenty
pleasured happiness
contently complacent,
bedded in rose petals.

Confirmed reassurance,
refreshing and quenched,
composing delight,
sustained,
remedied,
restored
and released!

Freely revitalized!

Snuggling cozy and sheltered,
pleasantly pacified,
      serenely secure. . .

Wake up!!!
Time's up!! You've been dreaming!
                      That'll be thirty-five dollars!
No checks please!
Feel better?
You should! Now I've got the change the sheets!

Indian Magique
(The History)

An early seventies tribe of upstart scruffy actors made theatre out of thin air; on a quest "to beautifully illustrate the painfully obvious." To the uninformed, they appeared to be or not, a bunch of standard issue, off-the-wall hippies, trying to get off on whatever they could. They had a plan.

This tribe, Indian Magique, was born into the drafty world of survival and uncertainty. They took to the streets for inspiration. Love gushed forth from a youthful fountain of sparkling energy. Their nation at war, and in a collective consciousness, they were reeling in the shock of déjà' vu. The children of peace were called to serve in a world falling prey to old ways. They gathered their wits and cunning in an attempt to carve out a small sliver of hope for a manifest destiny peace; to survive and serve as living examples of a new age of action. In the spirit of "the grandfathers", keepers of the flame, and as custodians of the earth, this small band of social warriors created a voice for their art, and gathered to share their hearts and their skills.

Through the haze of age, like fading photos bleed sepia into a treasured vault of virtual recollection, recall stumbles into an expansive third floor studio loft, 1974, downtown San Diego, at Fourth and Market Streets (now part of The Haunted Hotel). It is festooned with random cast-off keepsake costumes, props, set pieces, the significant necessities of abandonment, marking the home of the tribe, Indian Magique. Through the mist and the mold, a raging rag pile, one Alanowitz, in swim fins, crowned with a Viking horned helmet. He utters expletive nonsense to captive audiences, straining to decipher sacred meanings. The rag pile is upstaged by a hooded hunk of fat in tights, Bonzo, as he professes sweet vulgarities, in a most seductive way. Bonzo was the centerpiece of this cosmic bag of actors, and he was always shadowed by Bernard, who came equipped with a broad-brimmed floppy flaming hat and swash-buckling moustache, fit for the grandest rides, offered often and only to every tempting sweet young thing, who came close enough to be touched by his sensitivity; a bit of know-it all, and legend in his own mind, yours too, if you leave it unattended. Both assume alter egos as Swedish tuna hunters from the fjords of Sweden, closely pursued by an escapee from a gluten-free diet, Franz, who doubles as a crash-test dummy for anonymous seat fillers. He loved to wear masks, and pass himself off as a rutabaga in the broccoli patch.

Enter the confrontational chicken of Shabbat, Drewsch Bagg, taking the prize for the best potato croquettes in Kansas. He's the proverbial point man, always setting hidden minefields for laughter; impatiently waiting and baiting, where fools least suspect, to spring from his ambush with a "sucker punch line."

Approaches the angel apparent of innocence, Beaver, wrapped tightly in a twitching twit's countenance, suitable for gaming. A geek in fool's clothing, with matching mind-set, disguised as an unassuming chumpy door stop. Comes a skinny-assed biker, Wm. R, in a three-cornered hat, accompanied by a foul-mouthed young bag-lady, Henri, planted firmly on his lap. Smelling of gasoline, both bipolar possessed and, haunted by a Triumph motorcycle named Suzi which they ride to perdition, missionary style.

Two academic nymphs, Babs and Sally, who'd act for sexual recompense as everyone's sweethearts, playing dumb 'til it smarts. They lead all the young bulls by the rings in their noses, in a constant parade of studly hung poses. There was always a funnier way to do everything, and we had just the guy. Pouch never heard a better joke he didn't tell; he's always ready to argue what's funnier than funny. And who can forget the great director/producer, Mr. Scammie? He saw his future written in our tired young faces? He just needed a lift, and all our thunder to get off the ground.

I was the Sacque, dream-wizard of "What!" The quantomical psychic guide of this gifted brigade. I was taken hostage daily, by the flagrant disregard paid.

We are Indian Magique, the once and future players of this comedy set to life. We do it for passion, upon every altar, platform, stage, or anthill of perception. We met at the oasis, shared water at the well, and pledged to meet again, and still might. Someday?

Together we are the clown princes and princesses of theatre magique, the manifest of our destiny, the ones you want to be with, marooned in the depths of a lifetime, much like this; the magicians of laughter, something for nothing, and the vice of all versa, improvised, or rehearsed; to purge despair from misfortune. Just give us a bag of nachos and a six-pack, your troubles were about to begin. Nothing is safe, especially your imagination. We live to lift spirits to prominence, soar with angels, paying it forward in the love of our true coin of the realm, joy.

Subconsciously Bogart

A flash was heard upon the wall
as I crept into my ear,
and in my fur-lined bubble
an island in my eye did steer.
I slid through giggles
and smiled yellow,
to freak myself
in wet-dream despair.
Quite well spaced
and foaming mellow;
the curse of a bogart
who didn't share. . .

Born Out of Darkness

On September 8, 2011 Southwest America
                    experienced *The Great Blackout*.
This was my meltdown!

Blackout! All became blind in the night,
magnetically drawn to the bright on the thirteenth floor!
The Asian invasion comes muttering Mandarin,
seeking the light.
Disguised as a Boy Scout with fire,
I am Prometheus,
the eye with the mind for adventure,
and the light in the window of 1305.
Like fearless moths they dance to my flames.
And my light did so show!
I alone am the illumination of the nation in darkness!
Got a match?
A thought for your phosphorus;
bioluminescence, lights from within,
emerging from the ignorance of sin.
Differences forgot and forgiven!
The stolen-fire giveaway,
shedding omissions,
the candle of hope on a rope!
Pandora's promise, reborn into light again and again.
Stay cool while you blow, or whatever you do.
This one's for me, and that one's for you.
What do you make of that?
If you don't know, don't let it show.
We'll make a trade, 'just 'fore you go.
OK, spoil the surprise!
You want it all, I can tell by your eyes.
The one big problem, 'it don't come in your size.
Let's have a party, you get what you get!
Don't take the cake and then throw a fit!
Happy Birthday, you big baby!
You haven't changed a bit!

The Warm Bus

The bus was warm that December night.
There you are, the fair-haired goddess
                            of my most private dreams.
I should cast a clever thought, and start to talk;
but words have it sour with me, they evade my minds pursuit.
I take refuge in the silence, cloaking fears in breaking dreams.

How could I say I love you as I do?
Here sit I, fool years over, because I cannot create a victory
over wit and wisdom, beyond my throbbing paralysis.

Let me play your fool,
wet, warm, and sticky,
cream in your coffee,
kumming in quad,
in surges and flavors,
pricking delights,
one gushing wad
humping and thumping,
puffing and stuffing,
wherever it fits!

Like a Roman candle cannon,
I shoot out the moon,
as nymphs dance 'round the pole
in erect gushing twitches,
proclaiming new conquests and fame!

To hell with the bus!
Let's pull a train!!!

Gift Exchange

What do you want for Christmas?
What's the best gift of all?
Will it last forever,
winter, spring, summer, and fall?

What is that gift,
that makes us run, and jump, and grin, and smile,
that makes us laugh out loud, and want to fly a mile?

It comes with no instructions,
a game we know how to play,
one we'll play forever,
forever and a day.
It comes with optional equipment,
with balls and hats and gloves,
and dolls, and wheels, and flashing lights,
and all the things we love.

Sometimes, there are no parts,
or pieces to this puzzle.
It makes us act silly,
and feel all fuzzy-wuzzle.

Do you know, have you guessed,
the best gift to get and give,
by far, the very best,
as long as we shall ever live?

It doesn't even cost a dime,
everyone's most favorite gift,
we want it all the time,
it gives us such a special lift!

If you give up, I'll give you some,
and you give some to me.
Even though we go and come,
this was meant to be.

We all have to have this gift.
Nothing can stop us now.
If you don't want this gift,
well, you can have a cow!

If we didn't give or get it,
this season would have missed.
And, for every honest reason,
I'd be booed and hissed.

Take heart, my lovely children,
gather 'round this place.
Take each other's hands,
look in each other's face.

We can all share this moment,
with our family and our friends,
and help each other find it,
this gift that never ends.

We're only here a short while,
and shouldn't waste our time.
We need to get to giving,
and give meaning to this rhyme.

Fill your hearts with joy and laughter,
and unless I miss my guess,
you've just got and given,
that greatest gift called Happiness.

Can you say this word,
and feel the warmth inside?
Keep it in your heart,
Where it shall always abide.

Seized by the Moment

Vague recollection,
fades into fog.
An illuminated moment
sparks and flashes beyond grasp.
Shaken half-awake,
sleep-state deranged. . .
Slapped into reality
random resolve.
Outlines dim
hesitation to doubt;
arrested by gravity,
progress denied.
Truth slithers
to shadows.
My heart folds in half
lungs hiss and gasp
vaporous pain. . .
Head slams
the earth

beyond
pharmaceutical
redemption

and finality
in denial…

Words

Words that can hurt
words that can heal
words spread like dirt
words make thoughts real,

words without meaning
spawn mindless cause,
slant politic leaning
and mandated laws,

words give us action,
words stop us dead,
serve as distractions,
get trapped in our heads

deeds suffer shock
words rotten sour,
and talk has no walk
and purpose no power.

The Book of:
I-Say-Ah, One-Four-All

"Recovering in style, taking vacation, on denial,"
I said with a smile, as I crawl that last mile,
to the top of the pile of life's reconcile;
don't touch that dial!
There's still something to say!
Who's fooling the mirror with their perilous fear?
Time's growing near...
Contemptuous, straight standing, severe,
corn-pigeon-holed,
type-cast and rolled into some tidy mold,
the sum of the whole,
defined by the sex that we fiend,
the love that we make, the acts that we fake,
the drugs that we take, the tilt of our rake,
give me a break! You make my heart ache!
What does it take to be real in our eyes,
where all the lies fly in our face,
wrinkling into that place,
that trumps all our acts, makes up our facts,
and breaks all our backs?
We lie to ourselves, as we sit on our shelves,
in the do-nothing store, of "Go-Nowhere Galore."
Take your medicine, and go back to sleep; if you can...
We're so tired of the guise that veils our demise.
We never get wise, as our tub fills with lies.
Been done before, puttin' life on ignore,
that's how we got here!
To this! Not-so-sweet, not-so-dear, gripped in our fear,
jeered our last jeer, sneered our last sneer;
Excuse-Givers Anonymous!
Where we don't take any actions, make nothing clear,
listen attentively, but don't ever hear;
talk to ourselves, and, cry in our own beer.

While Old Wounds Bleed

Down perverted paths of glory,
you've come to show you care.
you've come to change the story,
to beat swords into plowshares;
here to make the world concede,
here to stop what makes old wounds bleed.

Burned out lights on moonless nights,
drowning in a sea of doubts,
probing eyes touch groping sights,
and you cry out, "What's this about?!"
And your good words are scarred by deeds,
and all good blood from old wounds bleed.

The world turned, now no where's safe;
in blood-hungry visions they slit your throat,
cast from the womb, an abandoned waif,
in sinking self-pity, you befriend the goat;
you offer your soul to survive with your needs,
now who's laughing while old wounds bleed?

Your spirit begins to fill with the pain
of bearing the weight of a double cross.
Paranoia found a home in your brain,
and all of your dollars can't fill the loss.
What once was compassion, now is your greed,
and it's your river of misery making old wounds bleed.

Fight to survive, and you'll succeed,
the signs are plane, or can't you read?
Man's demise has gone to seed,
no matter how you'll beg and plead,
helplessly drained, on you bleed,
'cuz you've sold out, yes indeed!

One Eternal Moment

Love has found me in your embrace,
and paid its ransom within the space,
of the moment living within our gaze,
touching dreams in magique ways.

Begin the touch and on it goes,
and in an instant, something grows,
breaking soil,
shedding light upon our toil.

We share a knowledge of one might,
then blind our visions from our sight,
and marry darkness in our fright.

Soar again, reach love's heights,
freedom speaks, a voice of lights,
shaking all the cosmos walls,
and on the burning whisper calls.

But common knowledge of our flaw
will wrench us back from what we saw,
to seal our memories with no recall;
there we cling to heaven's law.

Love is fashioned for a compassioned race,
and it has found me in your embrace,
taking us unto that place,
where the songs of living fill our space;
on to vanish, without a trace.

Angels Take Flight

From stillness falls silence.
Love's voice whispers,
"Follow me."
We bond to bear witness,
proclaim our devotion,
kindred spirits in the ocean
of eternal love, and light,
on this day of
declaration and confirmation
of noble omens of good fortunes.

Into sleek deep steep canyons
we float, gliding into place,
fold our wings,
behold the glow
of two blessed souls
to profess
the painful truth of love.
Two hearts in confession
of shared sacred dreams.
Purging souls,
to anoint in perfection
everlasting.

Every fiber, cell, breath,
and thought
caress, crown, and bless
the secrets of their hearts,
unto the heart of life,
within the heart of God,
as testament to a shared
boundless vision.

Love has spoken!

Honored and humbled
we share witness.

The universal mantra for all to
share freely in one chanted prayer
of covenant, love promised
from this day, forever.

As love grows and unfolds
to nurture, prune, and harvest
offerings of consecrated devotion.

Two promised and
willfully surrendered
in true testament
of transcending love.

You are the sacred bread
begot of divine
fire, earth, water, and air,
to become the heart of life.

Uncover naked joy,
eclipsing all doubts.

Love is sufficient only unto itself.

Direct not the course of love.
Love directs you,
only if it finds you worthy
to fulfill itself,
as you melt
to become
the gentle brook
singing in the night,

waking with light,
that emanates
from within,
giving love wings,
spreading the rapture,
as our souls sing,
every heartbeat
a new affirmation
of love.

Angels take flight!

From the Mire

                                              Transpire
                                      Respire
                                Expire
                         Perspire
                  Conspire
           Inspire
Aspire

                  From
                        the
                            Mire

You Know Better Than I

You should be me,
you know how I am,
you know how I think,
when I give a damn,
you know what I do,
you know what I don't,
you know what I should,
what I would, or I won't,
you tell me what's good,
when I'm wrong, or been bad,
or out of line,
or when I've been had,
what I should give, or how to receive,
what I think, feel, or believe,
my past and short-comings,
and how I deceive.

You should be me,
and I should be you,
that would be perfect,
I'd know what to do,
the way that you like it,
all things in their place,
just what you wanted,
me with your face.

Light-Blind and Abandoned

Ghost Dance reunion,
jump-start levitations,
possessions and trance,

this morning I pray for my enemy;
the door to the mind,
should only open from the heart.

Ha-ha cries the crow,
dove in the cottonwoods
call for the sun,
the curve of the land bends the light.

A shy wind whispered,
"Once the world was perfect."

Round ribbon sounds ride streaking sunlight,
embracing each breath,
begging entry to unguarded secrets
well aligned pretense in suspense,
sacred images perish,
forgotten in thoughts
of a moon stalking fire.

Light-blind and abandoned,
lost in a dream
of scorched treeless forests conjuring
grassless plains of mechanized sidewalk grazers,
aimlessly gleaning.
Curs'ed clock-watchers ambushed
in crossfires of a pointless continuum.
Every image fights to re-conceal vulnerability.

Screams fall on deaf ears. . .

Saint Jude's Prayer

Avow rainbow's aura in my mind's eye,
burdens of trespass unveiled secrets past.
"Dear Queen of My Heart, forgive if I die,
I am weak, and feel I have breathed my last.
My brother's keeper poisons sea and air,
having purged his neighbors with hateful flames,
our waters run blood, and he doesn't care,
amity crumbles to dust in our shame."
She spoke her heart, a tear crossed her pale cheek,
"My son, my father, my lover, my God,
conceit corrupts justice to ravage the meek;
love man, my love, guide the path that he trod,
for some day he'll know, to love means to live,
become the light, to fulfill and forgive."

You Were Once

Did you lose your drive to stay alive,
and pull over to the side of the road
to sing your death song?

Make preparation for departure,
giving notice to mankind and nature,
in a show of quiescent kneeling to repent,
holy rolling tones in tormented long laments.

Keening days of present futures past,
dies that never cast, having breathed their last
anticipated gasp.

Preoccupied finality utters last words of life
guided to the threshold by a smile, and midwife;
surrender to the pain and strife,
as you sever your bondage with a dull knife,
against the might of a random notion
sinking quick into churning commotion.

What prize fixed your eyes on such a thought?
To be, or not...

You do remember, but soon forgot,
when you got caught in your own ways.

Leave well enough rope to hang your fears.

Bid farewell this world awash in tears;

you were once, and then not here...
Never fear...
You were once,
and then...

Death Becomes Us

Driving Interstate 5
Camp Pendleton / U.S.M.C., CA, USA,
where we learn to kill,
flying down black velvet ribbons,
to an ever-changing tune.

Surfing songs for meaning,
through miraging moments,
swaying in the heat of day.

Where men made war,
and burnt the ground,
that made the hate,
that scorched the air;
death becomes us.

And someone laid a velvet ribbon
through the land.
And we ride the wheels
that burn the road,
and pass on by,
like we were never there.

The Daily Bread Excursion

There's no room for yesterday.
Like a bullet train that left the station, gone,
streaking into the darkening tunnels of our memories,
as they fade from the glare and fanfare of the here,
                                        and the now,
into the fog of when, and then.

Another round connived, as hopelessness arrives;
tears flush forth, through dismembered feelings,
drowning in a sea of lost embraces,
and discarded virtues of a prosthetic salvation.

Days rot into years,
with each breath come the fears.
You could live forever,
except for that secret that you think you thought.

The light leaks night into aces and infinite eights...

Strange glad-hands open empty.
"Give!" plead they.
"My all!" fools say.
"Not enough!" and away, with nine tenths of the law,
clenched fists crawl.

Strike back while the iron's still hot!
Amphetamines tumor, while stomachs rot,
waking to lie, living to die.
You shudder in pain with the knowledge of why
that monogrammed bullet melts in your mind,

leaving the familiar lagging behind,
left for dead...
Left and buried in my head...

Listen Jack!
'Bin smokin' that crack?
Every mother's son's
gotta keep it on track?

'Better pick up the slack!

I'm changing,
I no longer see, hear, taste, nor feel like I am;
but, I do smell.
Remember me well.

No earth is an island.

Come tempest seal the gap 'tween our form and vision,
make us one with the secrets of a rocking universe,
forging mountains, spanning light years
with exploding foaming brightness!

Christ returns gasping, grasping, clasping
the womb of sweeter moments.

"Going our way?"
"Wadayasay?"
"How 'bout 'a lift?"
"We just wanna get off!"

It hurts to much the other way; reality sandwich!
Random reality road-kill rapture,
as love's shadow drags her nails
across the chalkboard list of thoughtless deeds.

Who knows what anyone says
when we falter to alter our ways?

And the child lives,
but was never meant to stay young.

Angels, up and away!

What's wrong with loving,
even when it's wrong?
One flash is as good as another;
none better than the curse you utter.

The price of righteousness
is not easily concealed by lawyers or wills
as the wise plan their demise...

Good-bye cruel man,
taste of the bread sown in damnation;
for the sake of sinking synthetics
we've passed our brains.

"Here's to the end!"
Slick languid liquid fire, tempered in ire,
tricking the caverns, withering our glow
to the ash of our asses;
lost in some L.A. parking lot coin toss.

I saw it on T.V.

Dead-to-rights voyeurs replay the moment.

It's a right-handed world!
So, we're led to believe.

Decide to forgive,
and you're bound to receive
favor and purpose.

If you don't see it,
sit in the dark
with the debris of contempt,
bending the night with your cause to take flight,
with blind-shattering fright,
now cloaking our sight.

Hey, Mr. Cockroach!
How come you're always hiding?

Sheeeiittt!
You're just like some people I know!

Hidin's gettin' harder,
when your motive's well hid.
And you're hidin' what's done,
or rumored you did.

Nicotine breaths whisper alcohol prayers.
Holy words pass through holes in our souls
on way to their goals
through the muffled madness of more freeway songs
past the man on the cross
and the king of the goats.

Our spokesman has died. . .
We choked on his words.
He dropped on the floor,
swept out the door,
no more to soar the depths of mankind.

Well-practiced, we ignore,
using the tools of the trade,
all U.S. made.

Show us your wares!
See if we care!
So long, yet, so short,
just imagine the rest. . .

Pray with me. . .

Wake up uncertain,
wipe the nightmare from your face;
here comes the dawn.

Love is the light,
you are the spirit,
let your life shine.

You are unique!

Then gone. . .
Into the aftermath
of the perfect silence. . .

Returning
to
one
uplifted
prayer…
Free from every earthly care.

But for now,

fold up your wings,
open your eyes,
work your magic
with your hands
and your love.

Rebuild the temple.

Finish the job,
or,

at least die trying. . .

Amen

Every Word's a Prayer

Was it Greek to you?
Gyros with hubris?
Complimentary condiments smear through our thoughts,
the honeymoon's over! Juliet loved Romeo to death;
like the bums who coined "eye for an eye,"
those curious small beings, who burn holes in our souls,
and keep adjusting the focus on what we've been told.
One mean cuisine, topped with whipped cream,
just like this dream.
Depositing the incendiary load in the middle of the road,
where fracked captured rapture lay in spread-eagle Feng Shui,
before the Polo Gods prostrate in disruptive devotion
equivocating the balance of "To thine own selfie one for all!"
Harass mass societal outcasts back into our cells;
we're playing with fools, under fraudulent rules.
Restrain and retrain, autonomy lobotomy! Subscribe today!

Relax! It takes one to be.

Stay as good as you think you are,
right where you fell down,
in that genderless fear of naked submission,
cursing in colloquial Spanish your downcast upbringing,
with a burning desire, second guessing the devil,
while punching his time-clock,
growing defiantly feeble in protest,
losing each round with the smile of demise.
We'll win soon enough, and take our place in the sun,
all in neat ground rows, when clocks cease their concern,
where we hold all the cards, except, "the wild one;"
the joke's on us all.
So sorry! Really! Really?
We shall be known by the seeds that we've sown
in the end, we own all we assay, just to give it away. . .

ABOUT THE POET

CRYSTOPHVER R, a native of San Diego, has been involved in performing arts for over 50 years, as a writer, director, producer, actor and teacher of theatre, film, and video productions. He received a Bachelor of Arts degree in Directing from the United States, International University School of Performing and Visual Arts.

With a Masters in Screenwriting from the University of Southern California, School of Filmmaking, he has founded several theatre and production companies: Indian Magique, The San Diego Repertory Theatre, The Naked Shakespeare Company, The Bear State Theatre, and most recently, Yo' Mama's Got Drama Theatre Company. He also is a founder of a performance poetry group, The Mightier P.E.N.S. (Poetic Expeditionary Nation of Semanticists).

Crystophver is a past winner of The San Diego Film Festival in the professional filmmaker's division. In 2006, he received The Silver Remi Award in Screenwriting, from the Worldfest Film Festival, in Houston, Texas, for the adaptation of his play sequel to Shakespeare's ***Romeo and Juliet***, entitled, ***Mercutio, King of Cats***. In 1973, he received a special award from the BBC, as an "Independent Video Visionary." In 1996 his play, ***Bimbo Robots From Vegas***, won the Actor's Alliance annual play competition.

Recently, his poetry has been published in the *San Diego Poetry Annual*.

An accomplished photographer, he earned the top prize in The Senior Photography Exhibit, sponsored by The Park and Recreations of San Diego, 2019.

Some of his other works are *Crystophver R's Organic Groan*, a one-man performance piece, of poetical conscience, *Dead Sea Debris*, a play trilogy of fractured bible tales, *Ghost Dance*, a screenplay of events leading to The American Indian Genocide, *Cocaine and Able*, a day in the nightmare of a small-time drug dealer.

Currently, he teaches acting, storytelling, improvisational comedy, conducts poetry studies and readings for San Diego enrichment programs. He also directs for the San Diego Shakespeare Society, and serves as Producing Director of the Garden Theatre Festival, an annual event for the San Diego Park and Recreation Department since 2014.

Rproduction@live.com   yomamasgotdrama.com
intellectualsuicide.org

CREDITS

Cover and **inside title page**:
>*Crystophver R as Socrates*
>photograph by SOMER ROZE-POST

Back Cover:
The Mightier P.E.N.S.
left to right: Rudy G, Crystophver R, Chris Vannoy, Michael Turner
>photograph by SOMER ROZE-POST

Author:
back cover: photograph by SOMER ROZE-POST

interior: photograph by SOMER ROZE-POST

Interior:

iii	*Happy Buddhas* by CRYSTOPHVER R
4	*Crystophver of the 80's* by LEE CLARK
10	*The Ghost of King Hamlet* by LEWIS HIGGINS
23	*Love Slave* by MAUREEN MCNEESE
32	*R the Conjurer* by LEE CLARK
39	*Bagg Man* by SOMER ROZE-POST
52	*Ralph "Bonzo" Steadman* by LARRY PYLE
72	*Socrates Lives* by TORI ROZE
74	*King of Cats* by MERCEDES MURPHY
75	*Tybalt and Mercutio* by RICHARD SHARPE Chuck Wilson and Crystophver R
94	*Indian Magique* by LARRY PYLE **Top** (l to r): Bernard Baldan, Ralph Steadman, Crystophver R **Bottom** (l to r): Ralph Steadman, Frank Muhr, Hugh Monahan, Bernard Baldan
121	*Crystophver Magique* by LARRY PYLE
122	*The Lady's Poet* by LEE CLARK
123	*Being Shadowed* by CRYSTOPHVER R

ACKNOWLEDGEMENTS

Some poems in this collection first appeared in the *San Diego Poetry Annual.*

Made in the
USA
Lexington, KY